The Moon

Linda Aspen-Baxter

www.av2books.com

MEDIA ENHANCED BOOKS
AV² BY WEIGL™
ADDED VALUE • AUDIO VISUAL

Go to www.av2books.com, and enter this book's unique code.

BOOK CODE

M 4 2 7 0 1 6

AV² by Weigl brings you media enhanced books that support active learning.

AV² provides enriched content that supplements and complements this book. Weigl's AV² books strive to create inspired learning and engage young minds in a total learning experience.

Your AV² Media Enhanced books come alive with...

Audio
Listen to sections of the book read aloud.

Video
Watch informative video clips.

Embedded Weblinks
Gain additional information for research.

Try This!
Complete activities and hands-on experiments.

Key Words
Study vocabulary, and complete a matching word activity.

Quizzes
Test your knowledge.

Slide Show
View images and captions, and prepare a presentation.

... and much, much more!

Published by AV² by Weigl
350 5th Avenue, 59th Floor New York, NY 10118
Website: www.av2books.com   www.weigl.com

Library of Congress Cataloging-in-Publication Data

Aspen-Baxter, Linda.
 Moon / Linda Aspen-Baxter.
     p. cm. -- (Looking at the sky)
 ISBN 978-1-61690-954-3 (hardcover : alk. paper) -- ISBN 978-1-61690-600-9 (online)
 1. Moon--Juvenile literature. I. Title.
 QB582.K57 2012
 523.3--dc23
                              2011023439

Printed in the United States of America in North Mankato, Minnesota
1 2 3 4 5 6 7 8 9 0 15 14 13 12 11

062011
WEP030611

Senior Editor: Heather Kissock Art Director: Terry Paulhus

Weigl acknowledges Getty Images as the primary image supplier for this title.

The MOON

CONTENTS

The Moon can be best seen at night.

4

5

The Moon is made of gray rock.
It might have been part
of Earth long ago.

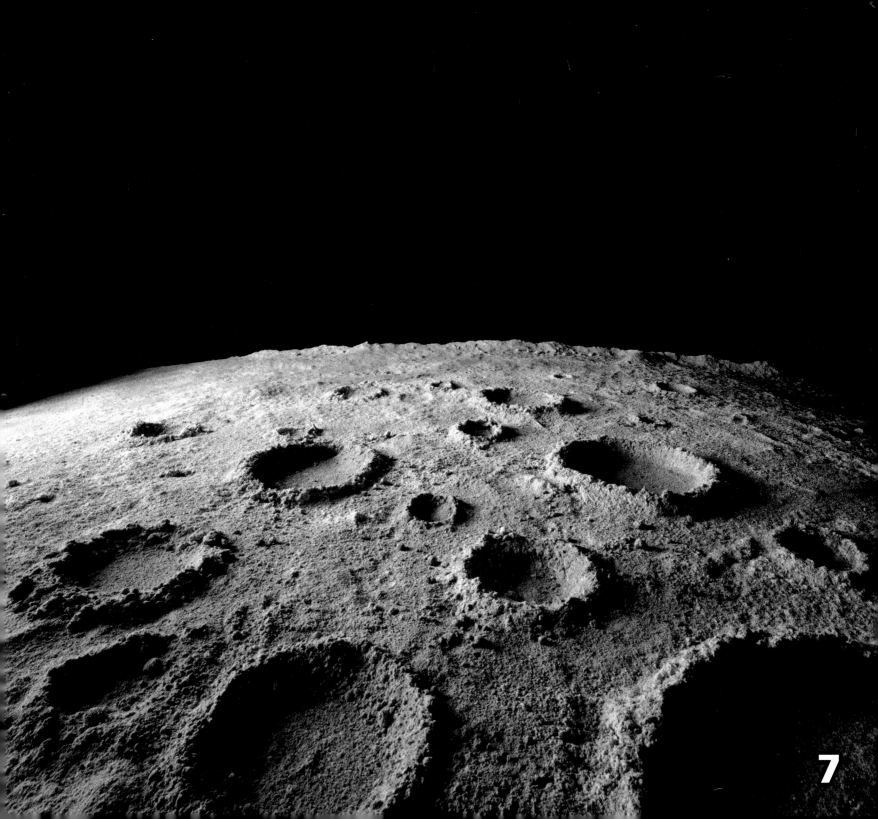

7

We can only see the Moon
when the Sun shines on it.

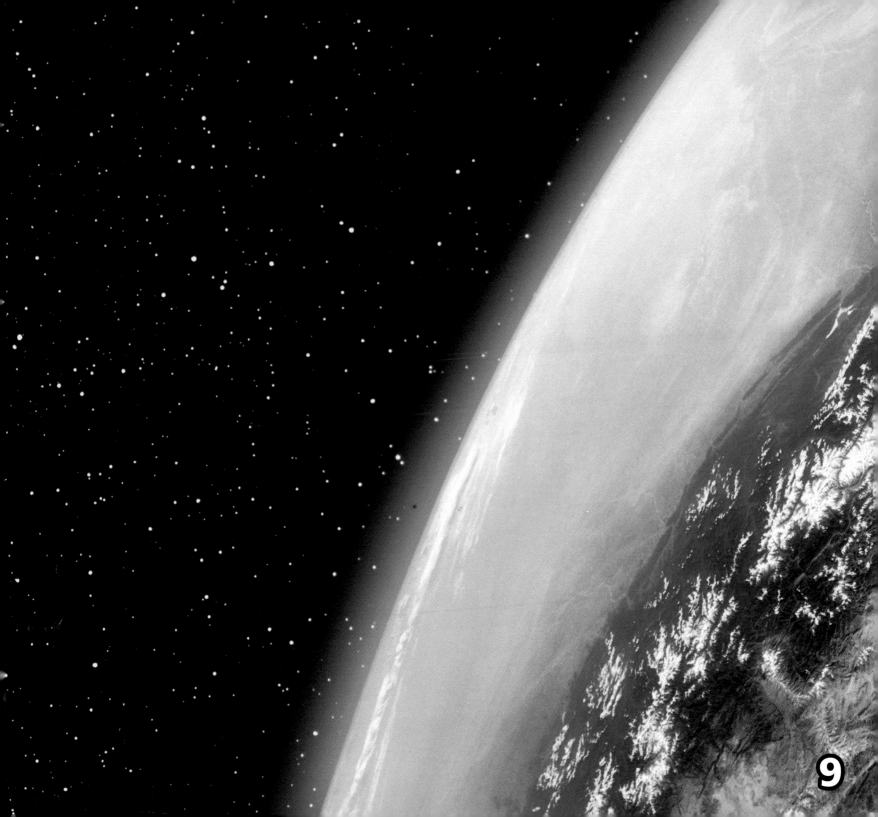

9

10

The Moon moves
around Earth in a path.
This path is called the Moon's orbit.

Sometimes, we see more
of the Moon than at other times.

13

14

Sometimes, the Moon moves between Earth and the Sun. Then, we can not see the Sun.

People first walked
on the Moon in 1969.

It took them four days
to fly there.

17

There is no air on the Moon.
People wear special suits
with air to breathe.

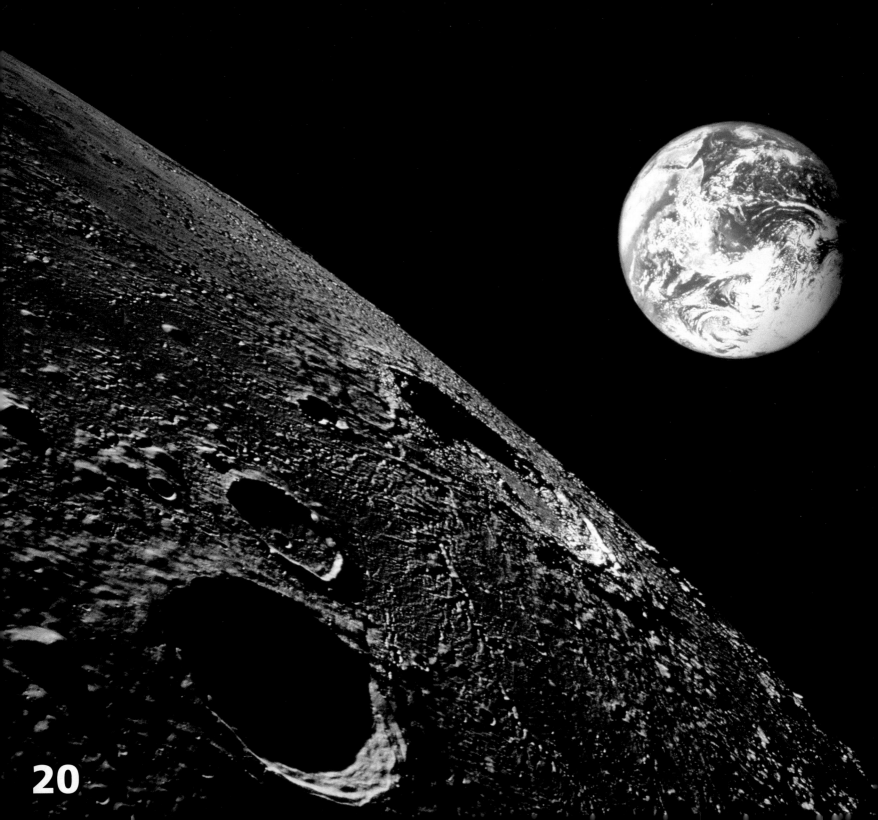

If you were on the Moon,
you could jump higher
than you could on Earth.

MOON FACTS

This page provides more detail about the interesting facts found in the book. Simply look at the corresponding page number to match the fact.

Pages 4–5

The Moon can be best seen at night. The Moon can be seen during the day, but the bright sky washes out the light that is reflected from the Moon. At night, we cannot see the Sun, but we can still see its light reflected from the Moon in bright contrast with the darkened sky.

Pages 6–7

The Moon is made of gray rock. It might have been part of Earth long ago. Many scientists believe that an asteroid struck Earth billions of years ago and chipped off a large chunk. This piece of rock began to orbit Earth.

Pages 8–9

We can only see the Moon when the Sun shines on it. The Moon appears to glow because it reflects the light of the Sun. The dark spots that can be seen on the Moon are low, flat areas called maria ("seas" in Latin). Brighter areas are called highlands, which are rugged mountains and plains. Craters dot the Moon's surface. They are formed when asteroids crash into the Moon's surface.

Pages 10–11

The Moon moves around Earth in a path. This path is called the Moon's orbit. The Moon orbits Earth about every 27 days. The Moon travels about 1.4 million miles (2.3 million km) in one complete orbit. It travels around Earth at about 2,300 miles per hour (about 3,700 km per hour).

Pages 12–13

Sometimes, we see more of the Moon than at other times.
When the Moon is between Earth and the Sun, the side seen on Earth is dark. As the Moon orbits Earth, the Sun lights up more of the side facing Earth. When the Moon is on the far side of its orbit, the side seen on Earth is completely lit up by sunlight. As the Moon keeps moving, the cycle begins to repeat.

Pages 14–15

Sometimes, the Moon moves between Earth and the Sun.
When the Sun, the Moon, and Earth are in a straight line, with the Moon in the middle, Earth experiences a solar eclipse. When this happens, the Moon is in front of the Sun. It blocks some or all of the Sun's light.

Pages 16–17

People first walked on the Moon in 1969. It took them four days to fly there. At 8:32 a.m. on July 16, 1969, NASA launched the Apollo 11 space vehicle. The crew landed on the Moon at 3:17 p.m. on July 20. About 6 hours later, Neil Armstrong and Buzz Aldrin became the first astronauts to walk on the Moon.

Pages 18–19

There is no air on the Moon. People wear special suits with air to breathe. Besides having no atmosphere, astronauts also have to be dressed for severe temperatures. It can be as cold as -280° Fahrenheit (-173° Celsius) at night, and as hot as 260° Fahrenheit (127° C) during the day.

Pages 20–21

If you were on the Moon, you could jump higher than you can on Earth. When people jump on Earth, gravity pulls them back to the ground. The Moon's gravity is one sixth the gravity on Earth, so when astronauts jump on the moon, they go higher. People also weigh six times less on the Moon than they do on Earth.

WORD LIST

Research has shown that as much as 65 percent of all written material published in English is made up of 300 words. These 300 words cannot be taught using pictures or learned by sounding them out. They must be recognized by sight. This book contains 48 common sight words to help young readers improve their reading fluency and comprehension. This book also teaches young readers several important content words. These words are paired with pictures to aid in learning and improve understanding.

Page	Sight Words First Appearance
4	at, be, can, night, the
6	been, have, is, it, long, made, might, of, part
8	on, only, see, we, when
11	a, around, in, moves, this
12	more, other, sometimes, than, times
15	and, between, not, then
16	days, first, four, people, them, there, took
18	air, no, with
21	could, higher, if, were, you

Page	Content Words First Appearance
4	Moon
6	Earth, rock
8	Sun
11	orbit, path
18	suits

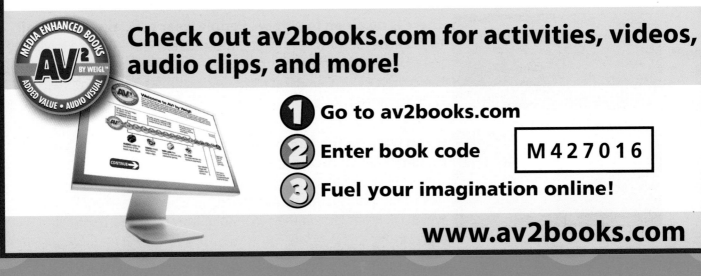